# Neanderthal Boy

## Colm Scully

*To Olga*

*Loved your poems.*
*Looking forward to reading*
*the book*
*Colm.*

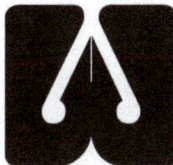

WORDSONTHESTREET

Published 2025 by
Wordsonthestreet
Six San Antonio Park, Salthill, Galway, Ireland
web: www.wordsonthestreet.com
email: publisher@wordsonthestreet.com

ISBN 978-1-907017-73-5

Cover design, layout and typesetting: Wordsonthestreet

Cover photo: sculpture of Neanderthal Boy by Isabel Scully

# Neanderthal Boy

## About the Author

Colm Scully is a poet and poetryfilm maker from Cork. His poems have been published in *Poetry Ireland Review, Southword, Cyphers, Crannóg, The Friday Poem and Orbis*. He has won the Cúirt New Writing Prize and The Deanna Tully multi-media prize. His short films have been shown at Cork International Film Festival, Fastnet Film Festival, The Bloomsday Film Festival and internationally. He teaches poetryfilm and is a creative facilitator with Cork County Council working in schools and libraries. This is his second collection and you can learn more about him at colmscully.com

Dedication

For my parents, Eileen and Don

# CONTENTS

# Alexandria

It could be mid-summer in Alexandria,
Eratosthenes* on his garden chair,
his dog dead-heading the antirrhinums,
chasing shadows along the tiles.
The first kumquats of an odd season
hang like oranges from waxed leaves.
A fluff ball dances above his head.
A bee charts blossom rivulets
as the Greek measures the breadth of the world.

Or you, two millennia later,
at seventeen on your school tour.
The deck awash with Irish schoolgirls,
their hockey screams as the boat docks.
Can I steal your memory for a moment,
freed by the nuns to wander streets;
meandering markets, curtained stalls,
Eratosthenes' statue on the hillside,
the ruins of the Amphitheatre and King Farouk's Palace.

The beauty of the gardens excites you;
a copper globe by the ticket kiosk.
You spin it on its axis,
letting Africa float across your palm.
There is a map there too, a reconstruction of his first.
That was the world then, there we are on the edge,
beyond Britannia, without even a name.
I see you now, searching for the indent,
The Bandon River, The Old Head of Kinsale.

## The Electrician

There's a sweet spot on his pliers;
with a squeeze I cut the garden wire
then wind it round the bamboo cane.

No matter what, I always find it
where the ridges meet, below the eye.
If a stranger tried it they would throw it aside.

But Dad always caught the cable
and spun the pliers gently
working it as a blade.

With a sharp pull he'd reveal copper
pointed, ready for connection;
blue, green and brown.

I retrieved it from his toolbox,
use it on occasion
and I'm no tradesman.

Still, if there are sunflowers to be staked
or a cable to be cut,
I'll grab its taped up handle and together
we'll find that sweet spot.

# The Otter

We walk on rain soaked roads.
An otter shuffles towards us,
her front paws dragging her load.

When I shout out *Is that a dog?*
she lifts her long neck,
her grey snout rising from ground to air,

her wetted fur sleek as salmon's skin.
She senses danger and shifts direction,
through ditch, down watery fields.

I turn to Isabel *Did you see her?*
Our eyes and ears sharpened from now on,
watching and listening, knowing she won't return.

# Irish Rain

There are no people in this country
who find the light too harsh,
like a grey mare, whose coat rarely shines,
except on winter roadways when the low sun blinds.

Rain falls on November through leafless branches.
Water berries cling to outstretched arms
holding the dull light,
filtered through mist that hangs on the day.

*Why do you all walk in the rain?*
an Indian friend asked once.
Now I see him push a buggy up a mizzled hill
wheels power-boating through puddles.

## Homo Sapiens Sapiens

When the Milesians came to Ireland
at the turn of the Ice Age
the Tuatha Dé Danann were here before them.
The Tuatha weren't half-god
as The Annals say.
They had stumpy feet and raised brows.
They walked with a constant stoop,
but had the use of fire and tools,
mostly bone axes and spears.
They painted on cave walls and standing stones,
concentric circles
closing in on themselves.

The Milesians were the last wave from Africa;
so many generations they had forgotten how long.
They had clothing and words,
crossing the land-bridge before the waters rose.
They stole ground from the Tuatha,
pushing them north.
As the last of their enemy died in the harsh winters
the Milesians told stories around the campfires,
drew circles on standing stones,
just as the Tuatha had done for ages before.
Where does the spiral end?
No one may ever know.

# Lord Protector*

The Irish are a degenerate race,
lower than the Scottish and the Welsh.
I am ashamed to say I have been with them.
Sometimes in this cold country
the warmth of a woman's skin can coax you.
Temptation, incarnate in blue black eyes, chestnut hair.

I stand now before the City of Cork,
Winter winds move west along the marshlands,
a most malign place, a most dispiriting site.
The affliction of the natives
is exasperated by the tribulations of the times.
They move, scarcely clothed, along the rough roads
to the outer reaches where the poorest keep hovels
in the liberties of Blackpool and Baile na mbocht.
These are the chaff,
degraded women and worker children
who make their way in the world through charring,
chopping, tanning and begging.
Picture them, not of the fat, savage tribes
that roam the hills with their cattle west of here,
but a subclass, brought to the outskirts of the town
by penury, without land or clan.

They serve the English well.
My host here, Coppinger, a loyal parliamentarian,
says they can work,
though gruff and unhealthy.
One served me at his table nightly
and answered my questions in English,
dressed in apron and petticoat
she resembled a London maid
but more ruddy and weather beaten.

There were no deaths here.
The population ceded easily,
being of a compliant, pragmatic disposition.
We fed on goose on Christmas Night in Ellis House,
then rode to service.
There are two fine churches, St Peter's where I knelt a while,
and Christ Church where all the merchants
lie buried in the crypt.
There we reposed for an hour,
the church itself being overly garish.
The local gentry and protestant classes gathered
but for my liking are too proud,
singing carols and hymns,
when solemness should be our earnest endeavour.

These are strange times,
I wonder why we need this place,
what purpose docs it scrvc?
How does it bolster England's goals?
I walked today along merging fields.
Those that are hedged, and that is but a part
have naught but cowslips and ragwort.
I even feel pity for the cattle,
munching at grass hidden among the weeds.
But they fare better than the natives.

I cannot see us gaining anything from this,
except to quell expectations.
They are all primitive papists
with mass stones and iconography their trade.
Crosses and virgin statues for sale on cramped city stalls,
beside yellowed cabbages and putrid cheese.
They've taken to planting potatoes lately,
brought by that vain privateer, Raleigh.
Its cultivation spreading west from Youghal.
It may in time become a staple,
suitable no doubt to feed and nourish the populace cheaply.

They are a childish race, a subspecies,
akin to the Indian or Negro,
part animal, part man.
You know this by their walk, their gait,
hair untrimmed, full of lice.
I was acquainted with a chief from Beara, O'Sullivan.
Brought before me at Limerick, as if I would sue peace,
or honour him as equal.
Beard to his knees, rough wool shirt,
deer fur across his shoulders.
Like some wild boar, brought in to dry by the fireside.
I think none of them can read,
more like the beasts in intuition than men.
Abandon it I'd say, set it loose.
Let this blood soaked land fend for itself.

As for the city, its islands and channels
have been compared to Venice.
In a dream,
less like the flooded plains of Lombardy than London is to Rome.
It's winter always, mist modulates the air,
all is wet and dreary, and no proper buildings stand
except those two churches I lately spoke of.

Oh to be in Essex now
along a snow lined path, bearing down on my home.
Readying my daughters for service,
reading The Good Book to my loyal servants.
But no, I'm here in Ireland
preparing for a new kingdom
of righteousness and glory,
one forever England.

# The Big Snow

*Do you remember the Big Snow?* I ask
You remember all of them.

Forty-seven,
horses pull coffins over frozen ground,
two weeks before a man can be buried,
the wells frozen, the army tied to barracks
while the turf ran out.
You're at typing school, Miss Lombards.
Making your way up Patrick's Hill,
your father's socks pulled over patent pumps,
digging your heels into the ice.
Shorthand copy squeezed under your arm,
dreaming of your first job.

Eighty-two,
ESB men out on the pylons,
soldiers deliver water off the back of trucks,
the Commons Road, a hundred meter ski slope
for fertiliser bags and school sacks.
You keep your youngest home,
a housewife twenty years, you hold the house
while we're off playing.
The mobile grocery van arrives
through heavy drifts with spuds and sausages,
your saviour from Fair Hill.

And then the last, 2018.
Schools closed for five days. No bread.
Queues for wine outside the service station.
You phone to tell us, *Stay indoors, don't cross the city.*
*The roads are treacherous, cars abandoned,*
*a child was killed in a fall in Farranree.*
*'Tis worse than forty seven.*
You're nearly ninety, your peers are dead,
you won't see weather like this again.
The slushy mountains thaw to black
along the road side.

# The Philips' Modern Atlas of the World

These are the countries of the world.
The atlas speaks to my ten year old brain.
Éire, Britain, East and West Germany,
The Soviet Union, Yugoslavia.

The book is covered in thick, green paper,
that also covers my bedroom wall.
I am understanding Europe
white capped mountains, earth brown coasts.

I trace my fingers across Asia:
Burma, Vietnam (North and South).
The straight and parallel lines of Africa:
Rhodesia, The Sudan.

Indented outlines of former nations
fade into contours and railway tracks:
Palestine, Montenegro,
Armenia, Kazakstan.

These seem to me beyond romantic,
elusive cultures lost forever.
The pages hold no hint of tragedy,
only of Kings and not their crimes.

I do not even try to imagine
that these states might re-emerge,
as I thumb through my new school atlas
safe behind suburban blinds.

# Morning at the Factory

Slow bowling in the gents' toilet.
As I approach, he drops his arm,
his mind deserting a Jaipur cricket field
for the lab bench and burette stand upstairs.

On the solvent tower a sample is taken.
A lone operator raises his head.
He looks out over Cork Harbour,
sings a single note to the scene.

The cleaning contractor vacuums the stairwells.
The Hoover glides across the floor.
Before work she painted her fingernails,
a perfect seahorse on each one.

The manager holds the door open for her.
He is daydreaming of heifers back in Kenmare.
As I pass them outside the gents' toilet
a crowd cheers somewhere, faraway.

# Yesterday's Wardrobe

When I was young
I had a pair of tan suede brogues
I thought were the bee's knees
and a grandfather shirt
bought in a factory sale.

I had a denim jacket
that I wore winter and summer
and blond curly hair
and I'd walk by the river bank
taking photos of the trees.

I had a woollen cricket jumper
that cost me sixty pounds
and a navy blazer with red silk lining
and I'd go dancing on Saturday night
with the boys.

*Shirt in or out?* I asked John T.
before the slow set started
as I scanned the floor.
Then put my bottle down
and asked you out.

The blazer's gone
the tan suede shoes,
the curly hair, and camera too.
The woollen cricket jumper
was never worn.

But you're still here,
and the grandfather shirt
still hangs in our wardrobe.
My mother told me,
*Never throw away your luck.*

## A History of the Pharmaceutical Industry in Ireland 1990-2020

All fine powder,
white, that ran through your hands
like dust from a sawmill.

No one knew the value of it,
only if it fell
fiery fits broke out.

I worked shift;
two days – two nights,
then days, then long days.

But the days grew longer
as the years passed,
till in my thirtieth year

the industry told me –
*You were the value,*
*you were the price per kg.*

# Smoke from a Chimney

February's last days wrap fog around the city.
Apartments dressed in red brick and grey zinc,
thick books and jotters scattered on a windowsill,
brown stone walls of the Diocesan Centre, weathered black,
high arched panelled windows revel in curious shapes.

A pigeon ruffles its feathers for no one
on the ridge above the high rise car park.
Below, the dipping slate roofs, push against each other,
amid ancient coach yards, bottling plants, hop stores,
turned funeral homes, waste ground, micro breweries.
The pigeon waddles along to the next ridge,
takes in the old city, its many streets, its shoe-horned manner,
its grey damp plasters, its bedsits and timber windowed rows,
letting change roll across its broken-glass trimmed walls,
its side streets, strung between new builds
and workmen's houses,
with brassed up door bells and turned over flower pots,
the unheard echoes of horses' hoofs clatter along its cobbles
clanging off tram tracks, bells ringing on the cold, still air.

Smoke from two victorian chimney pots,
rises over the houses, above apartment blocks,
multi-storey car parks,
and disappears into the grey, mist heavy sky.

# Ciutadella

I like small cities
the size of Cork
where you can walk around
and meet yourself again
coming out of the Bishop's garden
in Ciutadella
under the berber arches
by the ice cream stand
down slopes to the river
boat-sails quivering in the heat.
Towns not quite famous
where the fish market is a fish market
not just a tour-guide's coffee stop.

Those bigger towns
and tidy capitals
like Edinburgh and Ljubljana
– a tiny Paris
its river spanned by smart bridges
Museum, Parliament
and High Court
all in one square.
Cork size
comforts me.
I feel the sun's strangeness
but know around the bend
The Coal Quay, The Opera House
and St Mary's
or their exotic proxies
wait.

# Smells

Do you remember what Greece smelled like?
Going down to breakfast in the morning,
fresh yogurt and honey, the salt sea air,
oregano from the mountain.

Or in Athens, the hot tar rising,
rubbish at the corners and the baking stone.
In the ruins you could smell the dry air,
sun lotion from the tourists.

Or Africa, out in the bush,
the cheetah had our scent before we glimpsed him
through the broken undergrowth.
aroma of sundowners when we parked the jeep.

In Port St John it was a different smell,
mackerel cooking on open grills.
Reminded me of fish from long ago,
Friday, walking in home for dinner.

# Prayer to Saint Anthony

I could never leave the house without a holy medal
pinned to my back pocket.
St Christopher or Mother of Good Counsel.
Silver discs to keep me safe,
blue glass circled with latin script.

I found one on a ledge in St Mary's
during the Novena to Our Lady;
worn down pewter, St Anthony on one side,
windowed relic on the obverse,
a piece of cloth rubbed along his tomb.

It was someone's special pendant.
An old lady who placed it to her lips,
praying for her son's son
or the poor people of Russia,
now she searched frantically.

My mother let me keep it.
I moved it ceremoniously from pants to pants.
In school daydreams I'd run my finger along its edge,
reflected the sun off its face,
wondered where it had been.

I still remember how I lost it,
torn from my pocket in a game of war,
kicked into the earth.
Soon after I stopped listening for God's call,
stopped crossing myself when passing a church.

## My Uncle on a Sixpence

Lift up your head,

peep from underneath the covers.

What shall I wear today? The uniform of the

Queens guard, or the mantle of an emperor, called

back from the fields to save Rome. This valley and

village are my look-out across history. I've met the

world's men here. From royal doctors to long forgotten

heroes of the Mesopotamian wars. Six weeks in London,

and a few days in Killorglin, were enough to see both

sides of any coin. Those black-guards of republicans.

The righteousness of churchmen. The silliness

of women. Find a knight, and hitch your star

to his wagon. While I stay here,

awaiting your return.

# Riddle

I read
once, in a book,
it's saucer shaped.  Perhaps
a  chipped  one,  with  lots
of  hairline  cracks,  the  kind
you'd  pour  your  tea  into,  to  let grow cold
before  you sup  it,  with a soft  egg  and
soda  bread.  It's  quite  defined  in colour,
though  many  shaded.  It's  two but one.
It's  very  old  but  young.  It has a few names
to  describe  it,  in  different  languages,
one  seasonal.  It's  useless  in  the
kitchen,  but  can  be  found  in  the  odd
recipe,  always  associated  with  tubers
of  a New  World  kind. It's more
at  home  in  libraries  and  music rooms.
It's  comfortable  in  water.  In  fact, one could say,
it's  never  out  of  it,  which  is  uncommon within
its  family  of  objects.  It's  both a mother
and  a  friend,  It's  small  but  big. It's not
the  most  polite  of  entities,  rather
a  case  of  rough  around  the  edges.  It works
alone,  and  also  in  a  union, but has been used
by  others  in  the  past  for  their   own   ends.  It's
soft    and  hard,  and  can  get damp
quite  easily.  It's  demonym  is used
for  loads  of  things. From  any
angle  it  resembles  a   child's
toy,  in  side  profile.  Here,
hanging    upside
- down.

# An Alternative History of Ireland

Out of the mist of the Geraldine wars we emerged,
we became a travelling people.
It was a simpler way to survive the great skirmishes
between Norman Lords and English infantries.
Elizabeth was Queen then, and sent many English farmers
to settle and clear the lands.
We traded with them as we did with the settled people,
taking on parts of their language.

We lived at first in ditches, but as time went on we changed.
Taking canvas tents left behind by Cromwell's army,
while the poor farming stock lived in mud hovels.
That was long before roads.

We avoided the Round Heads, and came in after the battles,
re-using pikes and discarded implements.
We became tin-smiths, *Na Tincéirí*,
peddling our wares from townland to townland,
bringing news across the countryside to the people.

After Cromwell our numbers grew again,
as more and more became dispossessed.
For many years it seemed
that the wars between Catholic and Protestant would never end.
King versus King fought on the fields.
Our religion was that of the settled poor,
but at every step it lost ground.
The English brought in penal laws.
That did not bother us,
for we lived without land or house.
We had no churches, we taught our children as we moved along.
That was a golden time,
our way of life better than the farm labourers.
We traded and lived free
providing poets and musicians to the big houses
Gaelic, Norman and English Lord.

The Anglo-Irish ruled Ireland then,
with their parliament up in Dublin, Grattan and his men.
Many roads were built and that meant change.
We moved along them,
pitching our tents and feeding our animals.
We had our own kings.
We gathered at horse fairs, where our women met our men.
We traded ponies to the farming stock,
were storytellers to the townspeople.
But England was having none of it,
Ireland was growing too fat.

After the act of Union
our people did not prosper,
The settled folk lived on potatoes alone,
our special place among them was not so special.
We travelled further to trade, where the money was, to Britain.
We saw the Romany with their round barrel wagons.
We took to the idea and brought it home,
but here, there was once more devastation.
The potato rotted in the field and the people starved.

After the famine our numbers swelled again,
with paupers on the road joining us.
The labouring class had been wiped out,
and we were on the bottom rung.
It's strange how those left behind grew richer
buying out the farms they had rented for generations.
We were made welcome at the farmer's house,
but the new landed thought themselves better than us.
We still spoke our mixed tongue,
but they stopped speaking Irish.
Now, with their new status, it was as if many of them
were happy to have a foreign King.

But the old differences still persisted
and England feared agitation.

There was a great war in Europe,
and during it a small rebellion in Dublin.
They shot the leaders,
but the tide turned on England
and  suddenly we had our own country,
run by the rebels.

Our trades improved,
through the poor times that followed
but we had somehow became separate,
doing things our own way more than ever,
sulky racing, bare fist fighting,
moving to and fro from England.

And then at last prosperity came
after many generations of decline.
We swapped our barrel top wagons for caravans.
Shops and hardware stores were everywhere now,
selling plastic buckets from China for a song.
Farmers no longer needed gadgets fixed.
Our trades had to change again,
dealing carpets and sofas out of Hi-ace vans,
our women selling trinkets, reading palms for a few coins.

The people tired of us pulling in on their roadsides.
The rebels up in Dublin listened,
told us to stay put, built halting sites
with running water and electricity.
We took to travelling only in summer
when we could go to the old places, holy wells,
graveyards where our clans were buried.
We could light campfires, and our kids could run free.
But they told us we should stop that too;
*dirty caravans pulled in to industrial estates,*
*clothes lines blowing in the wind.*

Our work is gone and some of us have turned to crime,
stealing copper from old buildings and selling it on.
But we are proud to be Irish,
though the settled folk don't like us.
They think our children are lesser children.
They want us to disappear.
Their idea of freedom is boulders
strewn along the edge of roadways,
stopping us from pulling in,
stopping us from travelling.

# How Éire got its Name

The Milesians came,
long after the Great Flood,
landing their boats on the soft western sands
in the sickle shaped bay below the mountains.

They met and fought the Tuatha Dé Danann,
hunted them north,
till at the hill of Uisneach in the very centre,
a pact was made with Éiru,

*Yours is the land,* she said
*it has been prophesied long.*
*But you must promise me*
*that it shall carry my name forever.*

The first Gaels agreed
with the daughter of Delbáeth.
and the magic people were banished
to the rocks and dark places.

Every spring, on the feast of Bealtaine
the High King would marry Éiru again
at the Hill of Uisneach
to ensure a good harvest for the year.

# Stolen Memory

*(Monday 1ˢᵗ Nov 1920: Terence MacSwiney's funeral)**

We got a spot outside Alcock's, across from the Pavillion.
It was September, I remember, or October,
we were back in school anyway.
We left the tea and cake for after,
the streets were jammed.
Dad pulled me to his side, we squeezed to the front;
Bowler, long white rain coat, tweed jacket.

We waited, hoped the rain would hold off,
five deep on the pavement, all the way up to The Statue.
Trams stopped for the day,
cobbles had been washed clean.
We heard the clop of the first horses,
pulling a landau around the turn.
I remember someone shouted
*Seventy-four days.*
The driver wore a top hat,
embroidered sash across his chest.

*Who's in the first carriage?* I asked.
My father shushed me
as the second carriage came into view,
the only sound the clatter
of horseshoes over metal tracks,
the swish of reins to steady two black mares.
There were flowers everywhere,
climbing and crowning the second coach,
and two lines of men with caps
marched either side of the cortege,
each a wreath in his arms.

And the hatless men walking by the side of the coffin,
every so often one of them stepped out and was replaced.
Were they his comrades, brothers, or friends?

Then there was a third brougham, and a fourth, and a fifth,
carrying the top brass from the corporation and church,
with two riders on each carriage,
gold buttoned, top hatted.
*They must have used all the city's undertakers,*
my father whispered.

It took a full hour before the funeral passed
and the chattering crowd dispersed.

The Pavillion was full, we went to O'Brien's Dairy instead.
My Father smoked a cigar,
and chatted about the future to some men.
I had lemonade and a cream custard slice.
I remember thinking to myself
as I sat eating and listening,
*How could a man survive that long without food,*
*Seventy-four days?*

We had to walk as far as Douglas Mills.
We were picked up by Uncle in the pony and trap.
The day off school,
my younger brothers at home,
me allowed go,
because I was ten.

# Sliabh an Iarainn*

Rust stained clay,
amber streaked rocks,
gutted ridges scarred the mountain
where mortals mined the elements.

Beneath, smoke from the smelters
rose above the drumlin town
curling, intertwining
with the plumes of a dozen stills.

Coal from Arigna fired red,
fusing the ore to iron
while, below, smiths hammered out
the trellised frame
of the Ha'penny Bridge.

As we rise and watch
from our vantage on High Street,
the Georgian terrace,
the groggy smoker in a doorway,
the American widow walking her dog,

the clouds rise gently
from the mountain's peak
to reveal where the Tuatha Dé Danann
first set their feet down,
after descending from the sky,
to a virgin land.

Before Norman or Saxon,
before Viking or Monk,
before the Milesians swept in
to our western shores.

The why of their coming a mystery,
did they look back over their shoulders
to whatever doomed world they had left,
finding soft footfall at last.

# Neanderthal Boy*

These are the last few stretches of moor land,
beyond that it's the sea.
If I follow the coastline for two days,
I know there was a tribe of us in the hills.
My father brought me there,
taught me patterns of the land,
showed me the boundary lines with the humans
agreed in stone before the Gods.

I move swiftly, through the grasses,
my swollen feet tread only at night.
They travel in bands, I watch for them,
flailing spears stolen from us.
They used the boundary stones to attack us,
their hairless chests, their ochred eyes.
I break onto the beach when the moon is covered.
The Gods say someday they will turn on themselves.

# Sparrow-hawk

I

Until I nested in the woods above the factory I never knew men.
I'd watch them count their hours down outside the smoking hut,
watch as day turned, shifts changed.
I preen my feathers morning and evening,
peer down at them,
the load lifts from their faces as they pass out the gate.

Nesting is Springs work,
paper and string from the factory yard help in the making.
I await my mate's return, watch the sky.
Down below in the bike shed I see a man come at dusk,
the one who knows me.
His shift begins.
He locks his bike wheel and looks up,
sees me perched on the sweet chestnut's limb.
I measure his steps with my eye,
short and slow when entering, long when going out.

He never smiles, his eyes yellowed.
He is older, grey-haired,
the colour of my father's tawny wings.
How do they live so long?
I would not want it, struggling with weak limbs,
unable to fly to the mountain tops.

I snare a wren for supper tonight,
in the darkness I pierce his heart
then sleep on it.
Game is hard to get in these woods,
wire-ringed with the long factory fence.

My mate is late returning this spring.
Where are the two hawks born to us last year?
Out on the wild bog
living the free life.
These men who come through the big gate,
What do they work for?
What do they build?

Daylight wakes me.
There he is, finishing.
At his bike again.
Helmet on, dynamo light flashing in the daybreak.
He looks up,
knows where I build my nest.
Searching the treetop,
points it out to another who passes.

Across the sky and down over the estuary
I float on a warm up-draft coming from the south,
guiding birds homeward.
My eyes scan the mudflats for shrews and voles along the banks
but there is nothing here in the daytime.
On in towards the fenced factory I glide among the silent trees,
pigeons scatter at my coming.
There, down below on the path, one snagged on the wire,
a fat white-collared dove.
I am hungry today, I dive and hit her hard with my claws.
Shock strikes her dead, the rest of the flock flap wings on the
office roof.
Her blood oozes onto my talons.
I will have days of feeding here,
and leftovers for my mate's returning,
sure to be soon.
I beat wings and lift but she is heavier than me,
and caught in the wire.

I pull again, tear her flesh.
I cant't move.
Then, before me on the path, there he stands,
bike helmet still on, arriving for work.
Our eyes meet, he is unsure.
I try to rise, I cannot abandon my kill.

We watch each other. Stillness.
He moves off path, our gazes locked.
Taking me in.
I try to rise again, dragging at the pigeon's carcass,
feathers flying, flesh tearing,
no life in her now.

Still he stands, watches me
eyes alert, sadness lifted.

What will he do?
I can not let go my prey,
certain he will not harm me.

He knows I know him,
steps back,
and moves off footpath, watches me
then walks away.

At last I pull her free.
I rise with the heavy load,
first to a low branch and then to the nest,
now nearly fully built,
there I rest.

II
I have not seen him for days,
the car park empty.

Work has stopped and men with placards at the gate
bar the others from entering.
Cold last night, the clear sky and the darkness, no moon,
winter's last frost cuts into my bones.
Mist in the April morning burns off with the sun.
I am full from pigeon.


III
Fifteen days now they block the gate,
no steam from the chimneys, no one at the smoking hut.
My man is at the gate today, with a placard,
I saw him look my way.
His bike outside, against the fence.


The soft leaf-buds dress this old chestnut now,
the crows are in their oaks.
They avoid me, and I them.
I fly across the garden by the offices, a few men inside windows,
apple blossom hangs like snow on branches,
plum in purple leaf, come to life.
These days will bring my mate's song soon, and all new things,
I know it.


But here the air is still.
No men, no work at all the last few days.
They came in cars yesterday and went inside,
came out with bags.
Some moved slowly, others with a quick step.
Then a truck came and someone placed a lock upon the gate.
All things have stopped.


IV
He came this morning, and set his bike against the outside fence.
He found a place,
a spot with good vision, through the hedge.

I am angry, impatient from waiting for my mate.

I throw the ragged pigeon bones out of the nest.
He takes out binoculars.
He magnifies me, he thinks I do not see,
I watch him watching me.
He is calmer, the helmet is off his face
eyes are clearer blue.
I watch him smile.

Then, out on the horizon
a dot appears,
then grows, I hear a screeching, again it grows.
It floats as an eagle floats, wide wing span, gliding.
He's come.
I rise and soar,
circle the woods.
At last my mate is here, we circle together high in the sky.
We'll hunt tonight.

The man stares still,
watches us both,
I sense his heart singing.
He leaves his glasses down, retrieves his bike,
cycles away down man made paths.

# Argentina

After the  grasses
dance to the high wind,
after  the  pictures in  old  books
of gauchos, crouched around
campfires on the edge of a great          plain,
after the sun silk skin of girls picking ripe  fruit
in  summer,  the  edge  of  the  Andes
veined  in white,  clambering  to  the sky,
the  distant  dry  air  of  a  city  street,
the  tap  of shoes  to  a latin  beat  and
twirl of  dresses  trimmed  in lace,
after  the  Roman  word  for  silver
etches  adventure  in  my  schoolboy's
mind,  transports  me  to  a  land
young  and  bountiful,  to  a  place where
renegades  and  officers  ride  together,
after  the  generals,  the  heroines,
the  Villa  Miserias, the  runaway  inflation,
the  aggressors,  the  disappeared,
the  odd   film  in  an  art  house  cinema,
the  German  towns  haven to war  criminals,
the  striped blue  god-like  footballers,
the  wine  makers with  Irish  names,
I know nothing of you,
never  having
touched your soil
or walked your roads,
nor  of  your  culture,
save these few trinkets
collected along the path,
only that you are beautiful
and hopeful
and far away
and full of people
who every day
wake free,
or dreaming
freedom,
ready to take
on the world,
ready to
reach out
and
learn.

# Reprise

I remember a food trolley
at the edge of an orthopaedic bed,
preparing my copy book
for the incoming teacher.
School time
in the soft bone ward
and I am five years old,
mixing up my dees with bees.
But the stern woman with glasses
doesn't put me off.
The nurses are kind
and tell my mother on discharge,
*He was the best patient ever.*

Now, I fumble over words,
work hard but never excel.
All my life on the edge of ordinary,
hoping for a reprise.

## Meteor Storm

Shooting stars are out tonight,
you and I are watching them.
Blazes of dust, too quick for the eye,
or pinpricks, burning out slow.
We share knowledge in the dark;
The Great Bear, The North Star.
Something bigger hangs above
floating east to west.
How many nights do we get to see
The Milky Way dissect the sky?
It's a question God might ask,
scattered across the emptiness.

# Pigeon

I remember the people in my town.
There was Ten to Two, who walked like Charlie Chaplin
and Tabernacle O'Connor, the priest's favourite.
There was Giro, who stole a cheque from the Credit Union,
and Slab Sullivan, whose father ran the concrete works.
There was Beans and his brother Chips,
and Sunday World, who had all the news.

And then there was me, Pigeon.
I believed them when they said a bird
got sucked into the combined harvester.
They smeared droppings on my books in school
and flapped their arms when I walked by with my brothers.
I left town after secondary and went to work in Dublin.
When I come home I stay on the outskirts
avoiding the pubs and nightclubs,
afraid some local drunk will recognise me
and shout after me in the street.

# Tea Ceremony for One

Kettle boiled,
house empty,
I've set aside
this time to write.
The bag dipped
for moments only,
leaving the tea
see-through rouge.
A spoon of milk
turns it flaxen,
hot to the tongue,
I sip and watch.
An auburn store
of scattered leaves
sit silent on
my small field.
An old diary
empty pages,
the only sound
the fridge's hum.
The only motion,
a magpie parades,
samurai outside
my temple home.
I sit stone still,
master and guest,
lipping infusions
waiting for words.

# Vignette from the City

A garden on a flat roof above the Coal Quay
beds dug for spring, a polytunnel.
Laying hens peck in manure.
Below, a man from the council wheels his rubbish cart,
a beat rocks out from TKMaxx.
A Roma woman on a bridge begging
hums old songs to herself to keep warm.
In a cold doorway a blanket from the night before
trails in the mud of the wet road.
Vans deliver dough rolls to shop fronts
just lifting their rollers, clanging to a stop.
Two men on cherry pickers remove Christmas lights,
before the morning rush they'll get one more line down,
then off to the market for coffee.
Students from a dozen countries cross each other's paths.
A cat sucks at a drainpipe on Oliver Plunkett Street.
Ned at No 8 comes out his front door,
led by his bulldog,
nods to the people as he walks along.

## Cro-Magnon Woman

After the burial
we came down from the hill
and prepared a meal
in my brothers cave,
the children dragging and pulling
as I ground wild maize.

I thought of my sister,
the way the men tied her down
before crushing her.
I screamed at them to let her go,
cast her out from the tribe,
let her make her own way.

But they know better,
say mixing with the wild ones
could mean death for us all.
I gaze into my child's eyes,
remember my sister,
wonder where wrong comes from.

# Sparrow-hawk II

Torn from
daydreams,
in front of
me on the
path,  a young
sparrow hawk,
tawny  white
plumage, corn yellow beak, its talons
gripping a bloodied pigeon, snagged in the
fence. He tries to fly, dragged down
by the weight
he  will  not
abandon. Our
eyes connect
momentarily,
uncertainly,
in parity.

# Evolution

These days I remember things that never happened;
how the world was won
by us, through our evolution,
winning each fitness battle that we fought.

How we changed just the right amount
at just the right time;
watching carefully the giraffes growing their long necks,
watching the ants organise.

Still, now we can look with satisfaction
at the sacrifices made;
hairless winters without clothes,
the endemic sore back.

Oh, how we always picked the right solution;
the bigger brain over wings,
the opposable thumb over night vision.
Knowing deep in our psyche,
someday we would create radar,
someday invent aeroplanes.

# Saracens at the Gate

History metamorphosing into science,
clunk, clunk, clunk.
The gargantuan robotoid advances through the streets,
rabid dogs at its heels.

There is no place to hide
when history advances.
It moves innumerably,
like silhouettes across sand.

Once we were wanderers in the desert,
then Saracens at the gate.
Memories picked out of a line up
we are all in.

The esoteric machine crunches
living histories underfoot.
Obliterates nations,
metamorphosing into science.

Generating enthalpy,
perpetually transforming.
Dimensions its carrion,
spewing out obfuscation.

Clunk, clunk, clunk.
Villeins and serfs at a wake,
scientists collating information,
Saracens at the gate.

# The First Time the Pope Came

My mother came in Friday morning
to wipe away the condensation.
On the bus to school
my younger brother stood up front
chatting with the driver.
At the humpbacked bridge we all screamed
as the double decker leapt into the air.
Then the bus broke down, and we had to walk.
I had leather patches on the knees of my trousers.
Mother boiled red fish with milk and onions for dinner.

I picked fruit at Uncle's all Saturday long,
flicking helicopters in the air,
home in time for tea.
We said The Angelus at six
and the Rosary that night.
I polished all the shoes
for Mass on Sunday morning
then had my weekly bath,
rising my knees like hills, out of the soapy water,
wondering how the folks on TV got all the bubbles in.

Sunday morning we fasted an hour before communion,
watching the clock and gulping breakfast down.
Mick, the beetroot headed farm labourer,
threw his High Nelly over our fence,
when offered a lift to Mass.
Men hung around  outside the crowded church.
Afterwards, two lads passed
on their way from the bog,
bulrushes tied to their crossbars.
My mother bought a bunch
and placed them in a vase to Our Lady.

Monday, work and schools were closed.
Everyone was going to see the Pope,
except Uncle John and The Boomtown Rats.
I sat in the front room
and read about the Big Bang.
We loaded up the Ford Cortina
and headed for Limerick Racecourse,
walking two miles to where the vast crowds gathered.
I strained to see,
others had binoculars.
We stretched on tip toe and peered hard.
I saw the Pope-mobile's square podium
against the haze of heads
and nothing else.

# Purpose

There is no evidence for Purpose.
*Why* is a word for children,
part of a parent's toolkit,

scrambling to explain
the reason for things,
the beginnings, the ends.

But in stepping backwards
the unobserved past
becomes blurred.

All we see are shadows-
grasping at an answer,
hoping for resolution.

Our brains are built to ask questions,
resolve actions and reactions,
see cause in everything,

see time as progress,
an arrow aimed at a target
it was never going to miss.

Imagine no arrow or bow,
no archer or target,
time without edges.

We're still searching for purpose,
still asking a child's questions,
though there is no evidence.

# Interior Group Portrait of Penrose Family*
*(Robert Hunter 1776)*

My father's father's father came here.
My sons and their sons will depart.
Like a ship that passes beyond Hop Island
we will fade from the landscape without trace.

Those wild ditches I walked with William,
giving up pheasant, woodcock and snipe,
the long stroll to Elizabeth's home,
to meet our brethren, and to pray.

The fine house I built at Woodhill,
the quays on the river that bear our name,
all our good acts, the charity given
will simply be stories sitting on shelves

in Derbyshire or some such place,
accepting the remnants of our breed,
far from Grattan Street and the city
where once I strolled a merchant prince.

I thought someday we might number among them,
melt into their country, Quaker and Teague.
But our seeds never joined, the name never passed.
We left as we entered, only portraits remain.

# First-Hand News

I slip in beside the driver, my head groggy from stout.
Tonight I think I won't talk as I measure up the black
mumbling figure slouched behind the wheel.

Still, we start to banter about how quiet the streets are.
I tell him he sounds French. *No, not French,* he laughs
and talks about Nigeria, *a country that doesn't work.*

We wander down histories' lanes as an Afro beat plays,
he tells how the empire tried to cobble three nations together.
*I shouldn't be here tonight, cruising these damp streets.*

In rain slated Cork in winter I gather my most trusted news;
the Iraqi, who tells me about his bride-to-be in Baghdad,
the Afghan driver who warns, *Ireland had better pray
she never discovers oil.*

# Easter Monday, 1916

Some men have taken over the post office.
It is not right that they should interfere.
I remain at my desk as per Mr Keane's instructions.
I hear crashing and banging in the foyer below.

I write to you with regard to the franking machine
you requested for the depot in Eyre Square.
It was dispatched forthwith early this morning
before the current upheavals came to pass.

I enclose the engineer's letter for the said appliance
and a copy from London of the current rates,
please acknowledge received in working order
at your earliest convenience, but before week's close.

I hope you are all well in Galway,
give my love to your dear Aunt Kate.
A man with a gun has just passed my doorway.
It is quite frightening, I had best end now.

# The Old Soldiers of Killeens

They died in the ditches.
Not at the Somme
but in rural Cork,
a shell's arc from Shandon
and Collins' Barracks;
Dan the Man, Dinish Fleming, John Downey.

They knew of Gallipoli and the Ardennes
but lived to recount
tales to the farmer
in exchange for a few pennies
or a feed of potatoes and dripping;
three days work on the milk cart
or a week saving hay.

No army jobs for them
or posts in the civic guard.
No one to write or follow up
with the crown forces office in London.

They staved off hunger
with cheap stout in Caseys,
rambled the roads retelling stories
of the dead heat in Mesopotamia
or the souks of Basra
to the boys playing *Pitch and Toss*
at Killeens' crossroads.

They died in their britches
unknown and unloved
by Free State or King.
No poppies for them
at Windsor.

# The Neanderthal

Under the leaves of the orange tree,
that's where I met him.
Citrus shared between two,
counting each segment, he cut
the deep skin with his bone knife.
Slipping my fingers apart,
placing the fruit in the centre
then closing the cup.
So firmly he touched me,
leathery heat on my flesh.
I remember his words,
softer than man breath.

In the clearing they captured one;
my father, my brothers, their wives.
Pulled until limbs parted body,
I swore it was him.
Now I cup my fists
over my face,
chew on leaves of Bitter Melon
to remove his stain.

# The Seventy-Nine Villages that Disappeared off the Chalk Fields of Dorset Between 1348 and 1361

The English are away at war
fighting the French at Gascony.
A ship draws in to Melcombe Regis,
lowers her sails and discharges
a tired company of archers,
returning to family and fields.

Above on the chalk a boy is hoeing
the early shoots of spring corn,
he raises a hand to shade his eyes,
watches the sails flap and unfurl
beyond the Great Heath and the marsh
glistening below him on Weymouth Bay.

For ten years the plague is rampant,
the boats deliver death from France;
only this spring have people dared
to mourn their loved ones, gathered to pray.
His brothers have left this spade thin soil,
gone to the uplands for better wages.

He gazes up at the church above him,
Knowlton chapel's blanched white stone,
throws down his hoe and starts to walk
towards Melcombe Regis and the sea.
Behind him, his village disappearing,
archers are needed in Gascony.

# Rote Learning

My mother speaks in poetry,
quotes Othello and Laertes.
She tests herself at ninety,
can she remember lines
learned in national school,
or maudlin ballads
her father brought back from America?

She gets my sister
to search the web for distant volumes,
lost in the haze of syllabi.
Enunciates the words
with pace and emphasis,
turning up wisdoms
with each vignette.

Grown up grandchildren
indulge her.
Her own deflect as background noise
each sibilant verse
from Kipling, Goldsmith,
Hood or Longfellow.
She knows, but hammers on regardless,
returns to Shakespeare always,

*The quality of mercy is not strained,*
*it droppeth as the gentle rain from heaven*
*upon the place beneath. It is twice blest;*
*it blesseth him that gives and him that takes.*

At last I'm listening.

## Second Lockdown
## (November 2020)

Even in the sky the patterns are missing,
no soft white stripes, slow fading into blue.
Only a traffic plane circles overhead,
its waspish hum cuts the silence,
taking photos, mapping the pandemic.

Down here in the estate the sunshine
creeps over slated ridges,
brightening hedge tops and wall caps,
picking mottled condensate off roofs,
turning leaves to gooseberry.

Windows reveal little,
cast opaque by the sun's glare.
Shadows pass at kitchen sinks,
jumpered arms draw down blinds.
I step back, into my cell.

We're inside, five of us to four corners.
We meet at dinner. The youngest
has news from online school.
We talk about the numbers
and the chance of Christmas happening.

We go for walks together
and get caught in the rain.
A whippet nuzzles up to our dog,
sparks a conversation from distance
about tree hugging.

A Tortoiseshell lands on purple flowers;
disturbed, she lifts, fluttering,
her tangerines and burnt sunsets
more vivid than they ought to be.
I cut a sheaf of the long stems.

At home I rummage through old books
and find instructions
on how to make a lavender bundle.
My fourteen year old cuts and trims them,
sets with a blue bow on the windowsill.

# Syria

Syria sits in darkness,
our children locked in living rooms.
Women make their way to market
or wait at the food station.
The doctors have left for Europe,
the young men have joined the resistance.
Our Alawite friends have fled to Damascus.

A breeze rolls down the street by the kids' playground.
A barrel bomb sits in the sandpit unexploded.
Two French nurses walk by carrying a coffin.
The words of peace at prayer time seem empty.
The children of Syria are starved of the joy of being children.
How many have died in this war, I'm afraid to ask.
When the war ends who will be in charge?
They will tell us we need to rebuild,
to work together for Syria.

When my husband comes home this evening
from the university
I will say *tonight there will be no prayers.*
I am sick of praying and dying.
What can we do to end the war?

# Acknowledgements

Acknowledgements are due to the editors of the following publications and websites in which these poems, or versions of, first appeared.

Ciutadella, *Cyphers* 97 spring 2024, Pigeon, *Howl* Autumn 2023, Vignette from the City, *Poetry Ireland Review* 139 2023, The Electrician, *Skylight 47* Issue 15 2022, The Big Snow, *Crannóg* 55 2021, Riddle, *The Same Page Anthology*, UCC 2021, Sparrow-hawk II, *Local Wonders Anthology*, Dedalus Press 2021, The First Time the Pope Came, *Cyphers* 91 2021, The Otter and Stolen Memory, *Dreich*, Season 4 No 3 2022. Evolution, *The Friday Poem* February 2023, Meteor Storm, *Ofi Press*, Issue 49 2016, Syria, *I am not a Silent Poet* Website 2019.

The following poems have poetry films associated with them that can be viewed at colmscully.com:
*The Old Soldiers of Killeens, Interior Group Portrait of Penrose Family, A Prayer to Saint Anthony, Yesterdays Wardrobe, The Philips' Modern Atlas of The World, Purpose.*

# Notes:

P8, Eratosthenes was a Greek mathematician, based in Alexandria, who accurately measured the World's circumference in the third century BC.

P13, *Lord Protector* is in the voice of Oliver Cromwell.

P34, Terence MacSwiney was Cork's republican Lord Mayor who died on hunger strike in Brixton Prison.

P36, *Sliabh an Iarainn (Iron Mountain).* A mountain near Drumshanbo in County Leitrim, where myth has it that the Tuatha  Dé Danann first arrived in Ireland.

P38, *Neanderthal Boy.* There are many theories of the trajectory of human evolution. When I was writing the series of poems for this book on the subject it was thought that Neanderthal man co-existed with humans at some point. They may have been opponents in the battle for survival. Neanderthals, it is believed, died out, never cross breeding with Homo-sapiens. Some of the poems explore the possibilities of their interactions, through the personas of various protagonists.

P57, *Interior Group Portrait of the Penrose Family* is an 18th century portrait of a prosperous local Quaker family hanging in Crawford Art Gallery, Cork.